JFK

* * *

REMEMBERING JACK

by Christophe Loviny & Vincent Touze

SEUIL 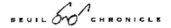 CHRONICLE

Originally published in France by Editions du Seuil/Jazz Editions in 2003 under the title *JFK.*

Copyright © 2003 by Editions du Seuil/Jazz Editions.

Original ISBN: 2-02-058939-7

English translation copyright © 2003 by Editions du Seuil/Jazz Editions.

Library of Congress Cataloging-in-Publication Data available.

ISBN : 2-02-059695-4

Manufactured in Italy

English edition translation by Peter F. De Domenico

Concept by Christophe Loviny

Design by Paula Holme

English cover and design by Vanessa Dina

Distributed in Canada by Raincoast Books

9050 Shaughnessy Street, Vancouver, British Columbia V6P 6E5

10 9 8 7 6 5 4 3 2 1

Chronicle Books LLC

85 Second Street, San Francisco, California 94105

www.chroniclebooks.com

PHOTO CREDITS:
John F. Kennedy Library: 5, 7, 9, 11, 13, 14, 15, 16, 17, 18, 19, 21, 22, 25, 27, 29, 31, 33, 35, 38–39, 45, 53, 73, 84–85, 87, 105, 118, 131, 135, 142–143. Toni Frisell, Library of Congress: 40, 41, 42–43. Jones, *Look Magazine,* Library of Congress: 47, 50, 51. J.F.K. Library, Robert Knudsen: 68, 69, 71, 81, 89, 90, 94, 97, 101, 119. Arthur Rothstein, *Look Magazine,* Library of Congress: 138-139. J.F.K. Library, Abbie Rowe, National Park Service: 57, 59, 83, 136–137, 141. J.F.K. Library, Cecil Stoughton: 63, 65, 66, 67, 70, 99, 102–103, 107, 108–109, 110, 111, 112, 113, 114, 115, 116–117, 121, 122, 123, 124–125, 127, 128, 129. J.F.K. Library, U.S. Army Signal Corps: 55, 61. J.F.K. Library, U.S. Dept. of State Photo: 75, 76–77, 79, 93. TimePix/Ed Clarke: 49. TimePix/Hy Peskin: 37. Zapruder Film/1967 (Renewed 1995) The Sixth Floor Museum at Dealey Plaza, Dallas: 133.

ACKNOWLEDGMENTS

The authors would like to thank the John F. Kennedy Library,
in particular Allan Goodrich, James Hill, and Jim Cedrone, for their invaluable
help and efficiency. Many thanks also to Maurice Hache, Megan Bryant of
the Sixth Floor Museum in Dallas, Radio KROC AM (Rochester, MN), and
Sherry Picker of TimePix.

On May 29, 1917, the United States had been fighting for two months in the First World War. In Boston, as elsewhere, army tents had been set up to enlist volunteers. In her house in Brookline, a rather affluent suburb, Rose Kennedy gave birth to her second child. For this fervent Catholic of Irish

"I tried to sublimate my discomfort in expectation of the happiness I would have when I beheld my child."

ROSE KENNEDY

origin, the birth month could not have been better. May is the month of the Virgin Mary. Rose had her bed placed near the bedroom window to benefit from the light. But there were complications, and the doctor needed to use forceps. The nurse administered ether to anesthetize Rose. When the little boy finally appeared at around 3 P.M., Rose was still unconscious.

John (Jack) on Rose's knee, with sister Rosemary (center) and brother Joseph (Joe) Jr. (left).

It was Rose's father, former Boston mayor John Fitzgerald, who announced the birth to the press. He was thrilled that the baby had been named in his honor. To his friends and family, however, John would always be Jack. Seven other brothers and sisters would follow, but the favorite would

"Dad persuaded us to work hard at whatever we did. We soon learned that competition in the family was a kind of dry run for the world outside." JACK KENNEDY

remain the eldest, Joseph, nicknamed Joe Jr. Older than Jack by nearly two years, Joe was an enterprising and self-assured boy who didn't refrain from asserting his physical superiority in brawls between the two brothers. In school one day, however, their IQs were tested. To their mother's great surprise, the results showed that Jack was clearly more intelligent. Rose later admitted having protested with the school at the time, believing the schoolmistress had made a mistake.

At the age of nine, Jack is a small, often sickly boy who loves reading, especially history books.

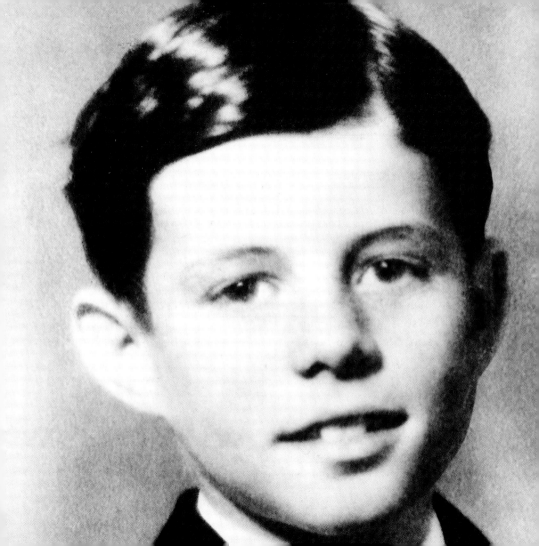

Descended, like his wife, from Irish immigrants who had fled famine and the oppression of English lords during the mid-nineteenth century, Joseph (Joe) Kennedy Sr. was a self-styled capitalist. Hardworking and ambitious, at twenty-five he was already president of a small bank; by 1924 he had become a

"The time came when we had to tell the children that their father was well-to-do. We were careful to emphasize that money brought responsibility." ROSE KENNEDY

millionaire, thanks to the stock market. He invested in the nascent film industry and, anticipating the lifting of Prohibition, bought back liquor licenses. In 1929, he was one of a small group of speculators who foresaw the impending crash. Having amassed a considerable fortune, he took an interest in politics and backed Franklin Roosevelt. The president appointed him chairman of the new Securities and Exchange Commission, a position in which he would come to regulate the very practices he himself had engaged in.

Robert (Bobby), John (Jack), Eunice, Jean, Joe Sr., Rose, Patricia (Pat), Kathleen (Kick), Joe Jr., and Rosemary on vacation in Hyannis Port, 1930.

Still in the shadow of his older brother, in October 1931 Jack followed Joe Jr. to Choate, a boarding school designed to mold the elite, based on the famous English college system. Yet Jack mocked the school's customs and drew attention to himself more through his rebellious spirit than through his grades. In his lectures to the students, the headmaster

"Jack has it in him to be a great leader of men. I have the feeling that he is going to be just that."

GEORGE ST. JOHN, vice principal at Choate

referred to such bad elements as "muckers." Right away, Jack and his band of friends founded a secret society, the Muckers Club. When their fraternity was discovered, the thirteen members were threatened with expulsion. Yet it was Jack's health problems that worried his parents most. Jack took numerous trips from the school to the hospital and back. The doctors couldn't agree on the cause of Jack's illnesses, and at the end of 1935—he was eighteen years old and had just been accepted to Princeton—went so far as to diagnose leukemia.

Jack (right) and three other "muckers," Ralph Horton, Lem Billings, and Butch Shriber at Choate in 1934.

Jack knew he was too young to die. On the advice of journalist Arthur Krock, he recuperated and built up muscles by working as a simple laborer at an Arizona ranch. In the summer of 1936, he won a major regatta at the Atlantic

"You ought to plan on seeing Europe before the shooting starts."

JOE KENNEDY SR.

Coast Championships and, when school began, this time opted for Harvard. By the time of Roosevelt's reelection, however, Hitler was already leading Europe toward another war on the other side of the Atlantic. On June 30, 1937, Jack and friend Lem Billings embarked for Le Havre, France. At the wheel of a Ford convertible, they spent over two months discovering Europe.

At Harvard, Jack (third from the left in the second row) belongs at the same time to the football, golf, and swimming teams.

"From Köln we headed for Utrecht on one of the autostradas, which are said to be the finest roads in the world—they seem, however, absolutely unnecessary in primary as there is very little traffic—however, perhaps Hitler in building them has something up his sleeve and is planning to put them to use for military purposes . . . Hitler's strongest weapon seems to be his very efficient propaganda."
Lem Billings

"We think him [the dog] a thing of great beauty, however, Jack immediately developed asthma and hay fever—so it looks like his chances of getting back to America are plenty slim."
Lem Billings

"Americans do not realize how fortunate they are. These people are satisfied with very little . . ."

Jack Kennedy

"On the way up Vesuvius we picked up two Germans— who turned out to be soldiers. They were wonderful guys— despite the handicap of not being able to speak anything but German."

Lem Billings

In March 1938, Joseph Kennedy Sr. was appointed ambassador to Great Britain. His diplomatic approach, however, differed from President Roosevelt's. A staunch isolationist, Joe was convinced that it was in the United States' interest to stay out of any war. In February 1939, after brilliantly pass-

"The necessary thing is not a solution just and fair, but a solution that will work." JACK KENNEDY, Palestine, 1939

ing his exams at Harvard, Jack was summoned to London by his father. He was introduced to King George VI and Princess Elizabeth, with whom he couldn't resist a little flirting. In mid-March, despite commitments agreed to in Munich, Hitler invaded the rest of Czechoslovakia. The ambassador dispatched his son to the continent to report back his impressions, from Paris through Warsaw to Moscow, then from Istanbul through Jerusalem (where the British were trying to remain neutral in the dispute between Jews and Palestinians) to Cairo.

Jack in Jerusalem,
accompanied by a
British officer.

Returning to Harvard to complete his bachelor of arts in political science, Jack chose "Appeasement in Munich" as his senior thesis topic. In his thesis, he considered England's blindness when faced with Nazi Germany

"I cannot recall a single man of my college generation who could have written such an adult book." HENRY LUCE

before the war. Arthur Krock encouraged him to publish the work in book form. With a foreword by Time/Life owner Henry Luce, *Why England Slept* appeared in July 1940, only a few weeks after France's debacle and just before the Battle of Britain. It was a best-seller. Jack was twenty-three years old.

Well before Pearl Harbor and the United States' entry into the war, Jack tried to join the navy but was rejected due to back problems. Finally accepted, thanks to his father's connections, he at first assumed tedious duties in the Office of Naval Intelligence. He eventually managed to study at the

"It was easy, they sank my boat."

JACK KENNEDY's answer when asked why he was decorated for heroism

Motor Torpedo Boat Squadron Training Center and took command of the *PT-109* in the Pacific. On the night of August 1, 1943, an enormous shape suddenly appeared on the port side. A few seconds later, the Japanese destroyer *Amagiri* nearly cut Jack's boat in two, killing two of the thirteen crewmen. Lieutenant Kennedy had to swim for four hours, leading his men to a small island. One of them was seriously burned. Jack towed him to safety with the strap of his life vest between his teeth.

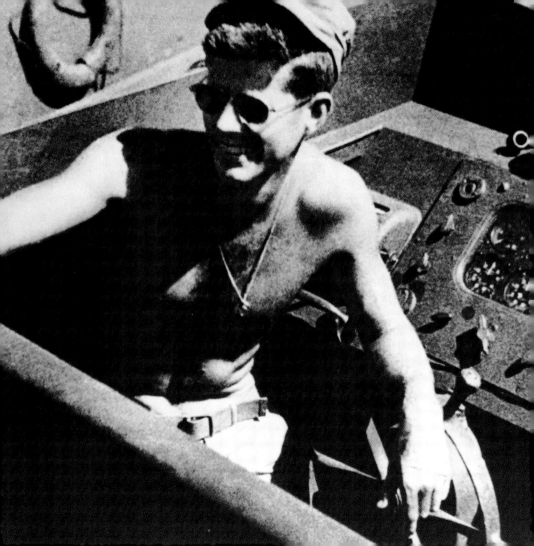

On August 12, 1944, Jack's older brother, Joe Jr., took off at the controls of the largest flying bomb ever designed, a Liberator bomber filled with ten tons of TNT. After the pilots ejected, the plane was supposed to be radio-controlled to crash into what the Allies thought to be the launch site of

"Don't force your luck too much."

JOE KENNEDY SR. in a letter to his eldest son

one of Hitler's secret weapons, the V3. But while President Roosevelt's son Elliott was taking photos of the Liberator from a reconnaissance plane, Joe Jr.'s plane broke apart in a tremendous explosion over Suffolk, England. In September, Lord Hartington, the husband of Jack's favorite sister, the bubbly Kathleen, was himself killed in France. Four years later, Kathleen would die in a plane crash.

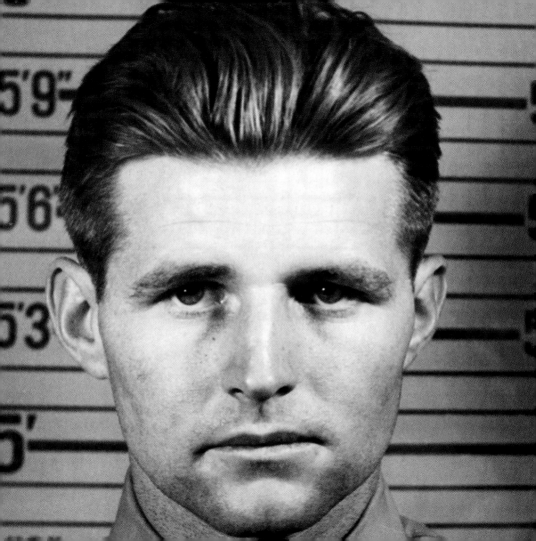

"O.K. Kennedys, let's go!"

BOBBY KENNEDY'S WAR CRY

Between a bout of malaria
and a spinal cord operation,
Jack relaxes with his brother
Bobby in Palm Beach, Florida.

"I was at a loose end at the end of the war. I was not interested in a business career. The first speech I ever gave . . . was given at an American Legion Post . . . Somebody . . . a politician, came up to me afterwards and said that I should go into politics, that I might be governor of Massachusetts in ten years. . . . Later in the fall . . . a congressional seat became vacant. This was the 11th congressional district which my grandfather had once represented fifty years before. Suddenly, the time, the occasion, and I all met."

Jack at twenty-nine,
campaigning in Massachusetts.
In 1946, he is elected to Congress.

As a congressman, Jack specialized in foreign policy. In 1951, he took a trip abroad with his brother Bobby. In Paris, the Kennedys met with NATO head General Eisenhower. The brothers next traveled to Tel Aviv, where they were received by Ben-Gurion. They then passed through Iran and Pakistan

"The fires of nationalism so long dormant have been kindled and are now ablaze."

JACK KENNEDY, upon his return from Vietnam in 1951

before arriving in India, where they were the guests of Nehru. On October 15, they landed in Tan Son Nhut, Saigon's airport, and were greeted by the sound of automatic weapon fire. Jack had a meeting with General de Lattre, a hero from the Second World War who was now battling the forces of Ho Chi Minh. When he took off for Japan, the young congressman concluded that the French would never overcome Vietnamese nationalism. Three years later, the French would meet their ultimate defeat at Dien Bien Phu.

Jack can be seen in
the group following behind
General de Lattre.

"We had 23 teas, to which between 65,000 and 70,000 women came. We concentrated on women because they do the work in a campaign. Men just talk."

BOBBY KENNEDY, during Jack's campaign for the Senate in 1952

During a television program, *Coffee with the Kennedys,* the clan mobilizes again to get Jack elected to the Senate.

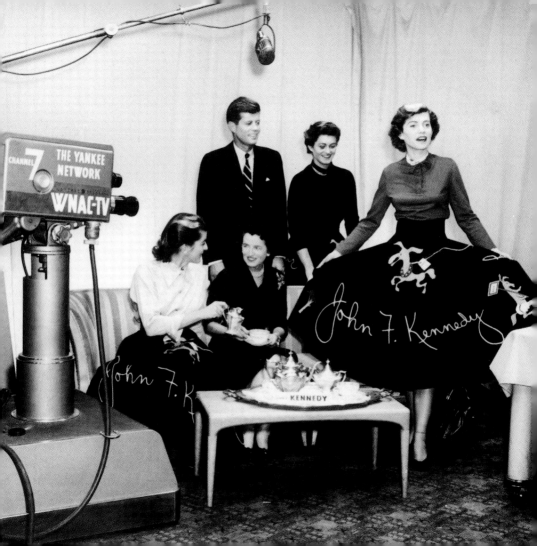

Jacqueline Bouvier was different from the other young women Jack knew. A graduate of prestigious Georgetown University after previously spending two years at Vassar, the most fashionable women's college in the United States, Jackie was not only slim and intelligent but had class, an air

"I leaned across the asparagus and asked her for a date."

JACK KENNEDY, during a dinner with friends

of detachment, and that little extra something that incited jealousy in other women. At twenty-two, she had already spent a year in France: first in Grenoble, the city of her ancestors, and then at the Sorbonne in Paris, where she had studied literature. She had tirelessly visited and revisited the Louvre, crisscrossed the capital by foot, and haunted the Café de Flore in the hopes of catching a glimpse of Sartre and de Beauvoir. By the time America's most eligible bachelor had asked her for a date, she was working as a reporter for the *Times-Herald*.

July 4, 1953. This would be Jack's and Jackie's first cover of *Life*.

Jack and Jackie apply for a marriage license. In May 1953, Jackie leaves for London to cover the coronation of Elizabeth II, the new Queen of England. Jackie's articles make the *Times-Herald*'s front page. Jack, elected senator several months earlier, sends her a telegram: "Articles excellent, but you are deeply missed. Love, Jack." Then, in another message, he asks for her hand in marriage.

Jackie recites "eeny, meeny, miny, mo" before tossing her bouquet.

"A crowd of 3,000 persons broke through police lines and nearly crushed the bride," writes a journalist from the *New York Times* on September 12, 1953. Jackie would have preferred a private wedding, but the Kennedy clan invites nearly 1,200 people to the reception thrown in Newport at the house of Jackie's stepfather, Hugh Auchincloss. From left to right, standing: Charles Bartlett, Michael Canfield, George Smathers, Lem Billings, Torbert MacDonald, Charles Spalding, the bride and groom, James Reed, Ben Smith, Joseph Gargan, Sargent Shriver, Paul Fay, Teddy Kennedy, Hugh Auchincloss II, Bobby Kennedy. From left to right, seated: Nancy Tuckerman, Martha Bartlett, Nina Auchincloss, Lee Bouvier, Janet Auchincloss, Ethel Kennedy, Shirley Oakes, Jean Kennedy, Aileen Travers, Sylvia Whitehouse, Helen Spalding.

In the summer of 1954, Senator Kennedy could get around only on crutches. He needed another spinal fusion. Moreover, he was also afflicted with Addison's disease, an ailment of the adrenal glands. Because of this, there was a 50 percent risk of fatal infection after surgery. But Jack

"Take any illness, Jack Kennedy had it. Many of them were painful. But I seldom ever heard him complain."

LEM BILLINGS

couldn't tolerate the prospect of being confined to a wheelchair and instead opted for the operation. Three days later, Jackie had to call a priest, who twice performed the last rites on Jack. He would need a miracle to survive. As president, Jack would impress people with his extraordinary vitality. But Kennedy would need to receive up to eight procaine injections in his back to be able to hold out during public appearances. His ever-present suffering could be discerned in certain facial expressions only by those closest to him.

Jack and his brother Bobby became television stars in 1957 during the broadcast of a congressional investigation into racketeering by the Teamsters. Bobby brilliantly conducted the examination of witnesses and grilled Teamster President Jimmy Hoffa for his alleged underworld ties. Named attor-

"This man Kennedy is in trouble, and he will get what is coming to him . . . he is going to be hit."

SANTOS TRAFFICANTE, Miami Mafia boss, September 1962

ney general during his brother's presidency, Bobby would pursue the Mafia vigorously, at a time when the very existence of organized crime was being questioned by FBI Director John Edgar Hoover, who was obsessed with the struggle against communism. Under the Kennedys, the list of mob targets in the Justice Department's sight for prosecution would rise from 40 to 2,300. Convictions would quadruple, arousing fierce hatred for the two brothers among the heads of the "Cosa Nostra."

Jack now weighed no more than 115 pounds. During his long convalescence, Jackie urged him to write a book, herself taking on the role of researcher. *Profiles in Courage,* based on the theme of courage in politics, was a bookstore success and won the Pulitzer Prize. In 1956, upon returning to the Senate, Kennedy tossed his hat in the ring for the Demo-

"Hi, I'm Jack Kennedy."

cratic Party nomination to the vice presidency. He was narrowly defeated, but emerged from this training run with greater stature. Every American from then on would recognize the irresistible smile of the young senator from Massachusetts. He was already dreaming of the 1960 presidential election and, while waiting, reveled in being a father for the first time. Jackie, after a first unfortunate miscarriage, gave birth in November 1957 to an adorable little girl, Caroline.

With Bobby's support, Jack throws himself into the 1960 presidential campaign against Richard Nixon. The two brothers employed very modern political tactics, dynamically exploiting the media to their own advantage. Crisscrossing the country in his private plane, Kennedy seeks to overcome his principal handicap, the fact of being Catholic in a primarily Protestant country. As Caroline's first words were "plane," "good-bye," and "New Hampshire," Jack named his twin engine in honor of his daughter. Jackie, pregnant again, only rarely accompanies him.

By taking up the cause of Reverend Martin Luther King, the unjustly imprisoned civil rights leader, Kennedy garnered the black vote. He argued for a more active and ambitious presidential policy and for a "New Frontier" to conquer. Finally, he scored decisive points against Republican candi-

"I expected to vote against Senator Kennedy because of his religion. But now he can be my president. He has the moral courage to stand up for what he knows is right."
MARTIN LUTHER KING's father

date Richard Nixon because of his ease during the first televised debates in history—an event for which he had prepared at length with his team. At 3 A.M. on the morning following the election, the results were so close that Jack went to bed without knowing whether he had won or lost. But the next day, little Caroline awoke him: "Good morning, Mr. President." He carried the day by a narrow margin of 118,000 votes out of 69 million.

"Ask not what your country can do for you—ask what you can do for your country."

January 20, 1961.
John F. Kennedy's inaugural
address, after being elected
President of the United States
at the age of forty-three.

The new president threw himself immediately into the problems of Indochina. In Laos, the royal army was retreating before the Communist Pathet Lao movement. Kennedy wielded the threat of armed intervention, but ended by negotiating a new coalition govern-

"In eleven weeks I went from senator to president, and in that short space of time I inherited Laos, Cuba, Berlin, the nuclear threat, and all the rest."

ment including the Pathet Lao. In the case of South Vietnam, he had to grapple with the Vietcong guerilla movement, supported by Ho Chi Minh's North Vietnam. The United States decided to reinforce the presence of American military advisers. Two years later, Kennedy also maneuvered to get rid of unpopular president Ngo Dinh Diem, but was shocked when a military coup resulted in his murder.

The president gave the green light in April 1961 to an operation initiated by his predecessor, General Eisenhower: the invasion of Cuba by Cuban émigrés, supposedly acting independently. Kennedy had faith in the CIA, which had succeeded in a similar intervention in Guatemala. At the same time, he

"I think the Bay of Pigs might have been the best thing that happened to the administration. . . . We would have sent troops into Laos if it hadn't been for Cuba."

BOBBY KENNEDY

held doubts and had the plans modified several times. This further complicated an operation that already completely underestimated the popularity of Fidel Castro, who had been in power in Havana for two years. The landing in the Bay of Pigs was quickly neutralized by revolutionary troops. It was a disaster that deeply affected Kennedy. Tempered by this experience, Jack altered his decision-making process and from then on relied less on his advisers.

Kennedy didn't admit defeat just yet. He suspected that the cold war was playing itself out in the postcolonial nations, and he felt it necessary to confront the Communists in the areas in which they excelled: secret and guerilla warfare. In late 1961, the CIA received the order to set up a vast destabi-

"The Romans' success was dependent on their will and ability to fight successfully at the edges of their Empire."

lization operation against Cuba, code named "Mongoose," which most notably involved attempts to assassinate Castro. The Special Forces recovered the famous green berets they had worn during the Second World War. The president also increased funding of this elite unit, commanded by General Yarborough, by 600 percent. Simultaneously, he created the Alliance for Progress in Latin America, which aimed to encourage economic and social development in countries tempted by the revolutionary Left.

JFK and General Yarborough,
commander of the Green Berets.

The Soviets made decisive gains in space. In 1958, they launched the famous *Sputnik*, the first man-made satellite. And the first man to orbit the Earth, on April 12, 1961, was a cosmonaut named Yuri Gagarin. Americans would have to wait until the following year for astronaut John Glenn to

"Can we beat the Russians?"
KENNEDY asks Wernher von Braun

become their first countryman to accomplish this feat. The president, furious that the United States was lagging behind the Russians, proclaimed on May 25 his ambition to send men to the moon before the end of the 1960s. He pinned his hopes on German physicist Wernher von Braun, who had been taken to America after the Second World War. But many doubted that the project could be achieved in such a short time. This is why Eisenhower, Kennedy's predecessor, had resisted making such a challenge. They were practically starting from scratch.

The first LEM prototype, the lunar lander, in September 1962.

Two weeks after Jack's election to the presidency, Jackie gave birth through cesarean section to a premature boy. Nicknamed John-John, the child suffered from an ailment of the lungs. Fortunately, he soon became a cheerful little boy, the darling of all America. When Jackie moved into the

"I don't want my young children to be brought up by nurses and Secret Service men." JACKIE KENNEDY

White House with her husband, her first concern was to maintain private space for her family. She intended to handle her children's education herself, insisting, above all, that they not be treated like a little prince and princess. Every evening she attended to their baths, pretended to dine in their company, and found her inner child again so she could tease and laugh with them. Jack and Jackie both had mothers who were stingy with their affection. Caroline and her brother, in contrast, basked in their parents' love.

On the fourth floor, in place of a solarium, Jackie has a nursery school installed for Caroline and the children of other White House staff. Once a week, she leads class herself.

"Hurry up, Caroline, I want to use the phone." The little girl plays hide-and-seek beneath her father's desk. The footrest is designed to alleviate the tension in the president's back.

On May 31, 1961, the presidential couple made an official visit to Paris. The crowd chanted "Ja-ckie! Ja-ckie!" They had eyes only for her. Even the ordinarily distant General de Gaulle was struck by both her style and her cultivation. He would later describe her as "a charming and ravishing

**"I am the man who accompanied
Jacqueline Kennedy to Paris."**

woman with extraordinary eyes." Kennedy felt a bit nervous at the prospect of meeting France's illustrious statesman and America's most irritable ally after the Bay of Pigs fiasco. Yet he was struck by the power of his wife. "De Gaulle and I hit it off all right probably because I have such a charming wife," he confided to adviser O'Donnell. Known for expressing himself only in French, the general even let slip a little English: "Did you have a good aerial voyage?"

De Gaulle was Western Europe's most important leader. His relations with Kennedy, despite numerous points of disagreement, would always be marked by mutual respect and sympathy. The French nuclear "strike force" under development, which threatened to breach America's monopoly, was

"Mr. President, you have to make sure Khrushchev knows you are a man who will fight." GENERAL DE GAULLE

a subject of contention, as was France's refusal of close British ally Harold McMillan's request to join the Common Market. During discussions, de Gaulle at the same time warned the young president against U.S. engagement in Southeast Asia and against any show of weakness before Khrushchev during the upcoming summit in Vienna. In October 1962, during the Cuban missile crisis, the general would prove to be the United States' most resolute European ally.

Jack stays in the king's chamber of the Quai d'Orsay, and Jackie in the queen's chamber. Dressed by Givenchy, her favorite Parisian designer, she has a distinctly royal look during the sumptuous dinner given in honor of the Americans and held in the Palace of Versailles's Hall of Mirrors. Later, when she appears with Jack in the balcony of the royal theater for a performance of an eighteenth-century ballet, the entire audience rises and gives them a standing ovation.

In Vienna, discussions with Nikita Khrushchev were neither friendly nor even cordial. The architect of de-Stalinization proved to be a resolute, intelligent, and cunning Communist, a fearsome adversary with coarse manners. The confrontation between the former *muzhik* and the Boston billionaire's

KENNEDY: "Our basic objective should be the preservation of peace . . . If our two countries should miscalculate they would lose for a long time to come."
KHRUSHCHEV: "Miscalculation! Miscalculation! Miscalculation! All I ever hear from your people . . . is that damned word, miscalculation . . . I am sick of it!"

son was brutal. The two men exchanged cutting remarks, during which the president used his sense of irony to his advantage. Faced with Khrushchev's intransigence concerning Berlin—the Soviet premier hoped to end the presence of Western powers there—Kennedy stood firm. But at the end of the conference, Kennedy feared that Khrushchev continued to underestimate him.

Once a reporter himself with the *Herald-American*, Jack Kennedy always maintained privileged relations with the media and counted many journalists among his close friends. This sometimes posed a problem. Ben Bradlee of *Newsweek*, for example, related that his friend, the presi-

"Well, I am reading more, but enjoying it less."

JACK KENNEDY, making fun of his critics in the newspapers

dent, never hesitated to chew him out when he didn't care for an article. He even tried to use him sometimes, which never failed to create an uncomfortable situation. Kennedy was a voracious reader. He devoured an enormous number of books and newspapers, thanks to a speed-reading technique he picked up early in his political career. He was the first president to give live, televised press conferences. His every appearance was a veritable spectacle for which he prepared very carefully.

Amused by White House Press Secretary Pierre Salinger's oversensitivity to the cold, Kennedy removes his coat and undoes his tie. "Now shoot this!" he quips to the photographer.

Although she despised being called "First Lady"—the term reminded her of a racehorse's name—Jackie took the role to heart. She had the White House refurbished, restoring its history, a source of national pride. When she first arrived

**"These things aren't just furniture.
They are history."**

JACKIE KENNEDY

there, not only was her shower broken but the many paintings and valuable objects that had historically graced the White House had been shipped off to a museum. She had to hunt down the masterworks at the National Gallery, secure private financing, and hire top decorators. Ever since her triumph in Paris, Jack had great faith in her abilities as a diplomat. In March 1962, he entrusted her with the task of winning over President Nehru at a moment when relations with India were especially tense.

Jackie's departure for
India and Pakistan.

During her visit to India, Jackie, accompanied by her sister, Lee Radziwill, takes a boat tour on the Ganges, whose surface has been covered in orange marigolds. An admirer sends her a letter written in his own blood, while an editorial labels her "Durga, the Goddess of Power." Everywhere, her photo is placed upon altars reserved for divinities. As for Nehru, he puts her picture up in his house beside those of his father and Mahatma Gandhi.

Jackie wanted the White House to reflect the cultural life of the era. In April 1962, she organized a dinner bringing together forty-nine Nobel Prize winners. The following month, French author and Minister of Culture André Malraux was the guest of honor at a function that assembled writers

"Artists invent the dream, women incarnate it."
MINISTER OF CULTURE ANDRÉ MALRAUX TO JACKIE KENNEDY

such as Robert Penn Warren and Saul Bellow, painters Franz Kline and Andrew Wyeth, and other figures such as Arthur Miller, Leonard Bernstein, George Balanchine, Tennessee Williams, and Elia Kazan. After dinner, the guests were invited to hear violinist Isaac Stern, accompanied by Eugene Istomin on piano and Leonard Rose on the cello. Later, Malraux whispered in his hostess's ear. As a gesture of friendship, he told her that France had agreed to let the Mona Lisa leave the Louvre for the first time for a January exposition at the National Gallery.

"JFK turned to his wife for advice whenever a crisis arose."

GENERAL CLIFTON, the president's military aide

America's Cup,
September 15, 1962.

In September 1962, James Meredith was the first black student to enroll at the University of Mississippi. Racist Governor Barnett attempted to oppose his enrollment, and Meredith was attacked by a

BOBBY KENNEDY: "Governor, you are a part of the United States."
BARNETT: "It looks like we're being kicked around. . . . I won't agree to let that boy get to Ole Miss. . . . I would rather spend the rest of my life in a penitentiary."

Telephone conversation, September 25, 1962

crowd led by extremists from the John Birch Society and the Ku Klux Klan. Jack didn't hesitate to send 12,000 federal troops. This victory in the struggle for civil rights left 2 soldiers dead and 166 wounded.

Kennedy loved the army and appreciated the company of soldiers. He particularly liked Chairman of the Joint Chiefs of Staff Maxwell Taylor, a former paratrooper with the 101st Airborne Division, who had jumped over Normandy in the early hours of June 6, 1944. On the other hand, relations

"Military policy and power cannot and must not be separated from political and diplomatic decisions."

were sometimes strained with other Chiefs of Staff, in particular Curtis Le May of the air force, a superhawk. Kennedy's presidency marked the largest peacetime increase in the defense budget. It would represent 10 percent of the GDP in 1963. And if nuclear forces were a priority, conventional forces weren't overlooked either. However, in Cuba, Laos, or Berlin, Kennedy demonstrated that he did not believe purely in military strategies, as threats or the use of force always remained for him merely political tools.

On October 14, 1962, a U-2 spy plane flying over western Cuba spotted launch pads for long-range missiles under construction. The Soviets had secretly been installing nuclear weapons on the island close to Florida, hoping both to prevent American aggression and gravely weaken

"This sudden, clandestine decision . . . cannot be accepted . . . if our courage and our commitments are ever to be trusted again by either friend or foe. "

JACK KENNEDY, televised speech on October 22, 1962

Washington's political and military position. Kennedy reflected in secret about how to respond. Some advised him to order an aerial bombing or even an invasion of Castro's and Che Guevara's island. But on the 22nd, when the president made the missiles' installation public, he instead called for a naval blockade of Cuba to oppose the delivery of offensive weapons and issued an ultimatum to the Soviets to withdraw the missiles.

On October 23, 1962, the president signs the proclamation establishing the blockade of Cuba.

KENNEDY: "If we attack Cuba . . . it would give them a clear line to take Berlin . . . which leaves me only one alternative, which is to fire nuclear weapons, which is a hell of an alternative."

LE MAY, AIR FORCE CHIEF OF STAFF: "I don't share your view that if we knock off Cuba, they are going to knock off Berlin . . ."

KENNEDY: "What do you think their reprisal would be?"

LE MAY: "I don't think they are going to make any reprisal. . . . I just don't see any other solution except direct military action—right now!"

KENNEDY: ". . . They can't let us just take out . . . their missiles, kill a lot of Russians, and not do anything."

**EXCHANGE WITH GENERAL LE MAY,
Air Force Chief of Staff, October 19, 1962**

Jack and General Le May in
the company of U-2 pilots
who had flown over Cuba.

The standoff would last a week. From October 22 to 28, 1962, the whole world held its breath. Nuclear forces on both sides were on high alert. For the first time, the planet faced total annihilation. Khrushchev at first stalled for time: While his boats didn't force their way through the blockade, he posi-

"We're eyeball to eyeball and I think the other fella just blinked." DEAN RUSK, Secretary of State

tioned his missiles in Cuba. On the 26th, he made an over-ture in a letter to Kennedy. The president, without yielding anything fundamental, responded with soothing declara-tions about his intentions toward Cuba and secretly accepted to withdraw technologically obsolete missiles from Turkey. However, as a U-2 spy plane was then shot down over the Caribbean island, preparations for an aerial attack intensi-fied. On the 28th, at the height of the standoff, Khrushchev cracked. The Soviets agreed to withdraw their nuclear arms.

The president with Chairman of the Joint Chiefs of Staff Maxwell Taylor and Secretary of Defense Robert McNamara.

"What kind of peace do we seek? Not a Pax Americana enforced on the world by American weapons of war. Not the peace of the grave or the security of the slave. I am talking about genuine peace, the kind of peace that makes life on earth worth living, the kind that enables men and nations to grow and to hope and to build a better life for their children—not merely peace for Americans but peace for all men and women—not merely peace in our time but peace for all time."

JACK KENNEDY, Peace Speech, American University, June 10, 1963

The president's favorite sports are sailing and golf. He adores taking the helm in all weather, and is indifferent to both cold and water conditions. On the golf course, as his back doesn't allow him to play an entire game, he plays only the most interesting holes. He goes out of his way to unnerve his opponents by cracking jokes and tangling them in complicated bets.

Ever since 1958, Khrushchev had been threatening to put an end to military occupation of Berlin by the former World War II allies. He considered humiliating the fact that East Germans were fleeing in droves to the West by taking refuge in the Berlin zones controlled by the United States, France, and England. After the Soviet

"All free men, wherever they may live, are citizens of Berlin, and therefore, as a free man, I take pride in the words *'Ich bin ein Berliner.'*"

JACK KENNEDY, Berlin, June 25, 1963

premier's threats in Vienna, Kennedy proved to be intractable, daring the USSR to act and calling up 150,000 reservists. Moscow didn't dare put an end to the quadripartite status of the former capital of the Reich. But in August, the Berlin Wall was put up by surprise. Regularly challenged since Stalin's 1948 blockade of Berlin, the Western presence was guaranteed from then on, but at the cost of a bitter status quo.

Foes of civil rights were powerful in Congress, and John Edgar Hoover was set on convincing the president that Martin Luther King was linked to the Communists. But once again, in June 1963, Kennedy sent federal forces to allow black students to enroll in the University of Alabama. The

"We preach freedom over the world . . . but are we to say . . . that this is a land of the free except for Negroes; . . . that we have no class or caste system, no ghettos, no master race, except with respect to Negroes?"

battle of Birmingham was a pivotal point in the struggle for civil rights. Governor George Wallace stepped up his racist declarations, while "Bull" Connor's police force attacked black protesters brutally. Kennedy responded by announcing major civil rights legislation, which would not be voted in until after his death.

During a White House visit, members of the National Association of Colored Women offer the president a portrait of Abraham Lincoln.

July 1963. Jackie is about to turn 34. She is pregnant again. The baby is expected in September. She and the children have taken up summer residence in Hyannis Port, this time in a house rented on Squaw Island and somewhat isolated from the rest of the Kennedy clan. Jack is on his way back from an emotional voyage to Ireland, the land of his ancestors, and is in the process of negotiating a treaty with Khrushchev to prohibit nuclear tests. He will join his family every weekend, spending time aboard the presidential yacht renamed *Honey Fitz*, his maternal grandfather's nickname.

Like her mother, Caroline is fascinated by horses. She regularly rides her pony Macaroni. John-John prefers driving daddy's convertible.

"Take my picture, Taptain Toughton." John-John, wearing his sister's sundress, asks the White House photographer, Captain Cecil Stoughton, to take his photo.

DOUBLE TROUBLE

On August 7, Jackie experiences violent stomach pains and is rushed to the hospital. Once again, she needs a cesarean section. It's a boy, Patrick. But the little preemie suffers the same lung ailment as John-John did at his birth. Jack uses all his power to find the best doctors. He watches over the baby himself, holding his minuscule hand to transmit strength to him. But just before dawn on August 9, Patrick's heart stops beating. "He put up quite a fight," Jack says, before taking refuge in the adjacent room to let his tears flow.

A week later, Jackie is able to leave the hospital and rejoin her family on Squaw Island. Jack has brought two new dogs, Wolfie and Shannon, back from Ireland for Caroline and John-John. The latter hasn't understood the drama that has just unfolded. Caroline, however, is still very shaken by the death of her second little brother.

When Jack visited Vietnam in 1951, he declared on his return, "I am frankly of the belief that no amount of military assistance in Indochina can conquer an enemy which is everywhere and at the same time nowhere." Twelve years later, he still seemed to

"It is their war. They are the ones who have to win it or lose it. We can help them, we can send our men out there as advisers, but they have to win it, the people of Vietnam, against the Communists."

hold this opinion, hoping to reduce the number of American troops in Vietnam, as he announced during a press conference on October 31, 1963. At this point, 16,200 men were stationed there and at least 82 had already been killed. In his mind, engaging the contingent was out of the question. But neither did he want to abandon Vietnam. The road was narrow.

Interview with Walter
Cronkite at Hyannis Port,
September 2, 1963.

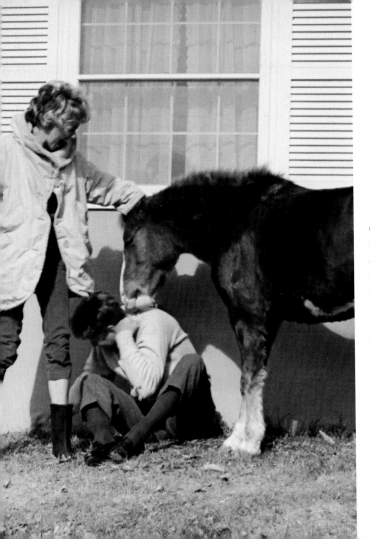

On November 10, 1963, the Kennedys and their children enjoy one of the last sunny days of autumn at their new home in Atoka, Virginia. Jackie has designed and decorated it herself. "Keep shooting, Captain, you are about to see a president eaten by a horse," Jack cries to the White House photographer who has accompanied them.

Caroline and John-John
explore the woods around
their new home, named
Wexford by their mother.
It's the name of the Irish
county from which the
Kennedy family originated.

In November 1963, Kennedy was preparing with confidence for the upcoming presidential elections. His popularity remained strong, even if it had dropped from 76 percent to 59 percent since January because of his support for blacks and civil rights. But a poll showed him gaining against

"My judgment is that by the time this Congress goes home, this is going to be a record in the fields of education, mental health, taxes and civil rights."

JACK KENNEDY, November 14, 1963

Goldwater, his most likely adversary, to 55 percent against 39 percent. In three years, major changes had occurred. On the cold-war front, the West clearly held the advantage. Kennedy could allow himself to extend his hand to the Soviets, who grasped it in turn, leading to the establishment of the red phone and a treaty prohibiting atmospheric nuclear tests. On the domestic front, Kennedy was undeniably held in check by Congress. But the time had come for major reforms, such as civil rights legislation and Medicare health insurance.

John-John is turning three. Like many little boys, he is fascinated by everything military: swords, guns, parades. "I guess we all go through that," his father says, a bit worried. On November 13, the whole family observes a parade to the sound of bagpipes by the Black Watch (Royal Highlanders).

Texas, which had voted for Nixon in 1960, was a crucial state in the upcoming election. In agreement with Vice President Lyndon Johnson, the president opted to begin his campaign there, and his wife offered to join him to support him. On November 22, 1963, at 11:40 A.M., *Air Force One* landed in

"You certainly can't say that the people of Dallas haven't given you a nice welcome." MRS. CONNALLY, the governor's wife, pointing out the crowd to Jack Kennedy

Dallas. Jackie emerged first from the plane, and the mayor's wife presented her with an enormous bouquet of red roses. It was a beautiful day. The crowd was cheering. Jack and Jackie, delighted, shook hundreds of hands before sitting down in the back of a Lincoln convertible, accompanied by Governor Connally and his wife. Around 12:30 P.M., the procession rolled at around thirteen miles per hour down Elm Street. Behind the presidential car stood the Texas School Book Depository building, where a certain Lee Harvey Oswald worked.

"Oh, no, no, no . . . Oh, my God, they have shot my husband! I love you, Jack . . ."

JACKIE KENNEDY, November 22, 1963, at 12:30 P.M.

An image from Abraham Zapruder's 8 mm film, four seconds after the first bullet struck President Kennedy.

Oswald, the alleged assassin, was himself gunned down two days later by nightclub owner Jack Ruby. The judicial inquiry never took place: a special commission appointed by President Lyndon Johnson and presided over by Chief Justice Earl Warren concluded that Oswald acted alone. But

"There seems to be some hard evidence of the second man—the second gun."

RICHARD BISSELL, former deputy director of plans, CIA

the commission and the FBI hadn't been driven by the quest for truth alone. Elements were hidden, such as Ruby's ties to the Mafia. O'Donnell, Jack Kennedy's adviser, had heard shots coming from a wall overlooking a grassy knoll. However, convinced by the FBI that he had made a mistake, he later changed his testimony. In 1979, a congressional commission arrived at the opposite conclusion than that of Warren's commission: "John F. Kennedy was probably assassinated as a result of a conspiracy."

After the gunshots, spectators throw themselves to the ground on the grassy knoll.

On November 24, a gun
carriage drawn by six gray
horses arrives to collect the
coffin at the White House
and bring it to the Capitol
where the funeral will
take place. The bier is
surrounded by five soldiers
representing the four
armed forces and the Green
Berets. One of them, like
hundreds of thousands of
men and women all over
the world, cannot hold back
his emotion. Following
Jackie and Caroline,
250,000 people march
silently as a final homage
to their assassinated
president.

November 25 is decreed a day of national mourning. On foot, Jackie leads the funeral procession across Washington, flanked by the remaining Kennedy brothers, Bobby and Teddy. They are followed by the rest of the family, President Johnson, royalty, and heads of state and government. The religious ceremony is celebrated in St. Matthew's Cathedral by Cardinal Cushing, who had married Jack and Jackie ten years earlier. Raising her eyes and seeing her mother's tears, Caroline squeezes her hand a little harder.

The president's remains finally reached Arlington Cemetery, where an immaculate blue sky was torn by the shrill sound of fifty jets honoring their commander-in-chief. Family and friends wanted Jack to be buried in Boston, his home state. But Jackie, backed by Secretary of Defense Robert McNamara,

"President Kennedy died like a soldier, under fire, for his duty and in the service of his country."
GENERAL CHARLES DE GAULLE

chose Arlington, the national cemetery for soldiers fallen in battle. Atop a mound, the site chosen for the tomb overlooks all of Washington. Prince Philip, husband of the Queen of England, used his saber as a cane to climb the hill. The entire White House staff was present, mingling with the dignitaries. The widow was presented the flag that had covered the coffin. With the aid of a torch, she lit a flame that is to burn for eternity over John F. Kennedy's tomb.

"Those who come after Mr. Kennedy must strive the more to achieve the ideals of world peace and human happiness and dignity to which his presidency was dedicated."
SIR WINSTON CHURCHILL

Jackie, Caroline, and John-John leave the White House for the last time on December 6, 1963.

SELECTED BIBLIOGRAPHY

Beschloss, Michael. *The Crisis Years: Kennedy and Khrushchev, 1960–1963*. New York: HarperCollins, 1991.

Hamilton, Nigel. *Reckless Youth*. London: Random House, 1992.

Kennedy, Robert. *Thirteen Days: A Memoir of the Cuban Missile Crisis*. New York: W. W. Norton, 1999.

Kennedy, Robert. *Robert Kennedy in His Words,* edited by Jeffrey Shulman and Edwin Guthman. New York: Bantam, 1988.

Kenney, Charles. *John F. Kennedy: The Presidential Portfolio: History As Told Through the Collection of the John F. Kennedy Library and Museum*. New York: Public Affairs, 2000.

O'Donnell, Kenneth, and David Powers with Joe McCarthy. *Johnny We Hardly Knew Ye: Memories of John Fitzgerald Kennedy*. Boston: Little Brown, 1972.

Reeves, Richard. *President Kennedy: Profile of Power*. New York: Simon & Schuster, 1993.

Salinger, Pierre. *With Kennedy*. New York: Doubleday, 1966.

Sorensen, Theodore. *Kennedy*. New York: Harper & Row, 1965.

Stoughton, Cecil, Chester Clifton, and Hugh Sidey. *The Memories: JFK 1961–1963*. New York: W. W. Norton, 1980.

Strober, Gerald, and Deborah Strober. *Let Us Begin Anew: An Oral History of the Kennedy Presidency*. New York: HarperCollins, 1993.